Atom Parlor

Joseph Bienvenu

To Maggie,

Joseph Bienvenu

March 17, 2010
New Orleans

BlazeVOX [books]

Buffalo, New York

Atom Parlor by Joseph Bienvenu

Copyright © 2010

Published by BlazeVOX [books]

Printed in the United States of America
Book design by Geoffrey Gatza
Cover illustration by Elizabeth Chen
First Edition
ISBN: 9781935402657
Library of Congress Control Number 2009910022

BlazeVOX [books]
303 Bedford Ave
Buffalo, NY 14216

Editor@blazevox.org

publisher of weird little books

BlazeVOX [books]

blazevox.org

2   4   6   8   0   9   7   5   3   1

B   X

Thank you to the editors and readers of the following magazines where some of these poems first appeared:

Big Bridge, Cranky, Glitterpony, H_ngm_n, Kulture Vulture, Mustachioed, & The Tiny.

The poem "Skymap" was included in *My Spaceship*, a chapbook from Cy Gist Press.

The poem "Let Me Pass a Cruel, Cruel Space" was included in *Machine Made*, a chapbook from Rhyming Orange Press.

Several poems first appeared in the chapbook *Pool Hall Quartet,* which was published by Verna Press.

Contents

White

Atom Parlor

Yellow

A Bigger Birdcage

Gunshot explodes into solar flares, enshrouds the city's histrionic heart in shockwaves of silent rodeos. The bull frozen in mid-toss is winking and counting out our days by the Chinese zodiac. Indeed there is no proof of technicolor continents, highway tunnels lingering beneath the tundras of tomorrow's sunken alibis. Shall we swagger through the strange beauty shows of pajama-wearing diplomats? Are we liars lost in gold lamé, false demigods of Korean soap? Let's laugh at obscene jokes while we plan our funerals. Let us shed the scales of our maritime dreams to place our ashes in the cargo holds of sunken submarines.

Border Patrol

Among the potholes and the citron haze, there is only so much to being alive, distracted by the brass spittoons and the pretended innocence of pregnant bartenders as the biography of dead French architects blares from the back room. Yet again my parking ticket is lost in the luggage; my winter coat is nabbed in some failed bank heist. It isn't hard to malinger in the little haunted spokes of college smokestacks, waiting forever for the half-baked forecasts, looking forward to the dense epiphany of valium in the bathysphere.

Kaboom

The sidewalk undresses its thousand eyes, tears open its shirt to find the drainpipe embossed with crescents. Skin is slowly reddening beneath the groans of imagined love affairs. Should I unleash my sticky fingers? Let my French cuffs flap? For who now talks of fate? —that feathered chorus boy of mathematical induction? The desert rises up here with a casual flick of the wrist beneath the black magma. The pocketbook lemons crushed beneath me. Huzzah! The funeral procession is dressed in corduroy. The periscope explodes the plaza's heart. The bricks sing out clandestine songs of women displaced by the sun with heads held high in avian masks whose boots are this afternoon's reason for living until I make my way home to the bedroom's ancient raffle.

Proliferation

Disc jockey of xylophonic sighs. The last conductor of weeping hand grenades, who knows how a bullet slips inside a sleeping heart. My equators are numbered in processions of Prime Ministers. My cabaret repeats the hoodoo of the sixth floor vomitoriums while my sculptor carves replicas of historic naval disasters. Yet my eyes are closed to the secret names of jellyfish, the calcified thumbs of countless river gods pulling apart pipes to find a hidden water leak, for whom the despair of lost car-keys occupies a millennium. How sad to be the terrible infection of French Parliament! The eternal mishmash of soccer match and the faint Ukrainian song. How sad to be marooned in the incomprehensible whirlpool of refrigeration supplies! To clamber upon the Corinthian guts of twitchy bicycles and junkyard radios.

Take a Look at the New Land

Monday's plantains salt our latest dreams, and the newspaper forecasts the diseased feathers of exotic birds. Once again I stumble into the latest drag show of the red lantern, the fiery breath of tomorrow's black umbrella. How much longer can I gawk at the exposed ductwork of my friend's gentrified apartment? Would it be less garish if she were here to entertain me? Or should I bide my time in Puerto Rican bodegas drinking Spanish wine? Should I write quatrains to the heat's English counter-tempo? Is it summer? Is it all the same? I am on the battlefront of honeybees who have wrapped themselves in the archeology of Latin rhythm.

Let Them Sleep

O 24 cylinder nightcap! O tongue behind the factory stammering into the future of some rinky-dink saloon. The libretto of ancient symmetries is now adrift in an aerial view of Lima. O days of hoopla! Precious science of calico! O brash Saturnalias of neon tubes inside the coat check where customers slip in for a peek beneath the out-of-body petticoats.

Minor Surgery

The squinty intersections of our ghostly selves echo in the honky-tonk of work-site radios. Perhaps our only blessings are tubercular, caught in the flimsy passwords of today's miniskirts. The washboard lit by the glow of the Ms. Pac-man machine makes us reconsider our callings. Scissors snip the tip of every wing, and the whispered songs of vegan clergy introduce us to our lives of crime.

Exhibition

Morning is consumed with tiny metal ampersands. Surge of
jet-skis fortifies the Richter scale. Woman diagonally
opposite, acid-etched into the tiles. Swami of persimmons
reinvents the guidebook in the shorthand of sleep. I bleed
the daylight in my urban chair. The giant eye and ear that
sprout from ashtray. Ice skate on primordial sea. Zinc bird
cage empties the banisters. At its heart the life-size cutout
of Japan. Slice of lemon discarded by high rollers at the
church bazaar. English language is a dust storm. Walk the
tightrope of the power lines. Do the peppermint twist.
Basilica equipped with female mannequins. Unearth the
public urinal with pick and shovel. Small schematic figure
of my spleen. Concierge is out to lunch. Morocco is more
difficult. Assemblage of smoke. Giant x-ray of the
minotaur. Grab the wheel with purple tentacles. Don't waste
time on clipping toenails. Frenetic oyster of the atom bomb. Split
and peel the shallots. Radiant pajamas hurtle past
construction site. Feel tongue stroking the palm.
The inevitable collapse of marshmallow. Wear a fur coat in the
summer's heat. Flock of sheep, thank you for calling me.
The objects in my pockets are talismans against the day
derived from liturgy. The stuffed owl soars through the
hybrid fantasies of microscopic cities. The Goodyear blimp
dislodges the illusion of fluorescent bliss.

Agent Yellow

Langolier flies to the moon. One more lemon drop plops beneath the heels of infant hurricanes. May my heart be powered by electric fan. On the corner, the oscillation of the engine of some damned delivery van is the only music I need. I'll grind the world beneath my microscope until I find some plain pretense for the day. As the last dollar wriggles through the hole in my pocket, the sclerosis of my backbone slips beneath the barroom religion of dice games, that good old funk of busted plaid. It's a harbinger of future's cruelty, the peppered light projected by the zombie sun.

Dilemma of Lemons

Around a parking meter, a garden hose is wound to form some ghetto caduceus. And I'm caught in the rain with canvas shoes, another slight disaster of the solar plexus, governed by the Spanish dancers in my head. Leave me in the corner of some ill-lit basement, and I'll tend to my own health. The afternoon is filtered through the hum of restaurant machinery, and my pockets are full of silt. My medicine is the sadness of geology. The faces half-obscured by columns remind me of forgotten friends, and the earaches of conquistadors echo in my bones.

The Afterglow of Sonic Boom

At the bottom of a well, you leave me to dwell
on more important things. I am breathed upon
by the flapping of wings: a pigeon well
versed in fluttering. How soon
the sky would shed its lucent skin to light
upon a dancing girl I cannot help but spy
in the lobby bar in the hotel in the night.
A polished brass banister she brushes by
with which her skirt would have its little flick,
and my heart not holding a card case, traveling
only with people, I think of a cymbal,
a slow wheel I am likened to.
I will probably end up choosing none of these,
propelled like a flood of lightning,
the shower come in again after a storm
like me for nothing, after all,
just a glance down a hole.

O Perfect Yellow

O last gasp of available air
O monorail
propped up on hidden supports
It shook
O building I come across
with terrible weather
O teeth
pink cellophane
O unaccounted for thought of the past
O shape of an eggplant
O dark-haired girl in a taxi
O mathematics
shock waves of silence
O face covered with hair or the hood of her jacket
O basement
O lime I might eat
green carpet
O medicine of life
O sleeping giant
cooling duct
O lamps along the river
O let the dogs
move freely through the streets
O second-hand parrots a lot of whom are pink
O number on the door of a rented room
I change to a set of escalators
O the words we
can't say about women
O gorgonzola
O flashes of the landscape
If I knew I think I might stop
O the blue of industrial smog
beautiful as glaciers

Blue

I Walk and Walk

Back and forth between myself and burning building,
blue lady behind sparks
like an almost perfect illusion of Venice.
Also the artificial sky is worth mentioning
because it makes me forget
we have to burn it finally down,
burn fragrant wax.
On the horse I ride,
the legs represent the front legs (one pair of stilts)
are drip-less
in the midst of brokenness.

Sing along with me the night
and clean flint cullet.
The moon almost immersed in the umbra—zebra-like.
Yesterday I cried
for myself or for something I can't remember.
Under this sky of silver foam
what is this river upon which float
the kayaks of legs in black stockings?
Legs that go white at any mention of the day,
legs that anticipate caresses.
I see legs rise and fall like sheets of carbon paper.

Eyeing the Behemoth

I go down certain streets and cobras flash Basque jackets. Collarbones collide amidst the glaze of ancient idols whose many arms are occupied in digging up weeds, whose many hands apply sunscreen to the backs of beach-bunnies, whose skin is the blue of cardinal sin. Each simple syrup is a spoonful of sublime monotony. The tiger rises again in a solo whiskey rebellion, an explosion of cacti. Will the virgins guard the Vestal flame against assaults of hipster hordes? Every hobo vagabond is eclipsed by polka-dotted silk, is crooning turban-headed into plastic buckets, composing soundtracks for the gypsy panhandlers, is howling pornographic operas for the waitresses on damaged pedestals.

Walking through a Muddy Place

Oh to pass my life in vague aquatic dreams,
one pale blue dot beyond,
and not make my way back to the above ground "land-station."
I slip a bit who sings and prays
and gazes into slot machines.
Maybe anything will do.
Whatever we seek there is nothing.
The longer a person holds on to a lamppost, the greater the change in its color.
Like a cat in heated swimming pool,
I end up jumping in the air to sing
a song that's far too frail,
tropical bird song.
I hate it,
but I slog right through.
A possum had come to rub its chin on the bower of my stoop
because I loved him slightly less
than the boy over there with the broken leg,
green corner of the garden of my fingertips,
a place I can only reach when everything is white,
when my lips hurt really bad.

Let Me Pass a Cruel, Cruel Space

Orb that glows beneath the ear.
Faint pink scallop of blood.
Can I not to stroboscopic skies uplift? Must I slash in bows
against her skinny ribcage tied? Field forced open. Light
emitted through woven glass fibers. Transatlantique.
I leer upon a world like a flood.
Tapping Belgian sportswear maverick, what would I have done?
From the tower didn't the curve of the city ebb
into metropolis? Didn't telescopes focus on a tremulous calm?
How sweet to me the must of rain-soaked canopies.
The spinnaker of a sailboat grinds the flesh of an impossible disease,
rots out my gut and plays host to the metallic dust of
white arm gleaming through the trees like a restaurant
where diners sink away beneath the billows of the leaves.
What feathered curve of darkened skin might squirm out beneath green
cotton capelet and quash my voice. The train that loops around itself,
clings to an upside-down surface, is one more mechanical fragment of longing.
I, a little darker than the blue around me, I began when I was new,
was a basilica of the mere past so no one noticed the refuge of my spiral staircase.
The sun never rises. The sun never sets.
For whenever beauty is pressed, like a swimmer rising to the surface
with veins caught in the weight of his chest, pooled at the end of undivided
consciousness, never resting in our field of vision, it only waits for interruption.

Futuristic Scene

Yes, the city is measured in geologic time: the frozen suicides of streets where asphalt is replaced by moss. The explosions of blue under layers of darkly tinted glass. But how long until the waters build up in quiet cul-de-sacs? I am one more innumerable victim of a diving accident where head wounds blossomed into brilliant orange. If I stop to pray beneath the red onion dome of the church on Baronne, it is too late. Thousands of young argonauts amass in the museum to lounge on leather fainting couches where a fire has broken out. Cheekbones aflash in a hollow blue blaze of light. Take me to the airport. It's here and then it's gone. Only planes remain in smoking alabaster heaps. There aren't even any bridges or rivers, just futuristic scenes in abandoned warehouses and ruined factories. See, the sun has set and still I can make out the tops of the temple pylons, the naked white body of the railway lines. I look longingly at the lithesome lines of riverbeds. I had no idea about the teeth, how everything is white from afar. I would like to see the many wonders I have never seen. I will measure the exact distance from the oil refinery to the building around which endless trains meander. What use is this map of places that no longer exist? Who will be at the Monteleone tonight? Who will sit at the bar and write elegies to forgotten saloons? I am in the sky, and I tip my hat to the sad refrain of peacocks crying over steel guitars. I will tell you what it means to lose what is always and everywhere present. I would like to die while the moon lies like a lion on the sandy floor, while the city grows higher and more luminous. I would like to live in this place like a priest.

Revolution Boogie

O the night might shoot the finger of the artificial spleen as the moving vans
wear out the evening's villainy. The sun sets only on the half-baked, the deflated
tires on the fat girl's bike. And if I point my beetle boots towards the North
Star, I'm still the pimple on the cinematic eye, the continental drift that spins
the blue bladder of unintended destinations, the self-appointed volleyball of
this bleak and grizzled beach.

Verandas and Viewscapes

O rotten life beyond the Japanese lanterns! O to shuck oysters in the aimless blue time zone of the avant-garde snuff. Why is the summer heat not peeling off its wrapper to reveal its limpid lady heart? Is it off secreting kisses from kimonoed dancers in cathedralled alleys? The camera is obscura, but how can it be silent? The Bienville shimmies its hips up to the finish line, a bit of razzle-dazzle that distracts the eye while I slide down banisters forever. No one even sees the wires. Should I cry real tears for the laundromat lost in the overgrowth of leafy canopies? It might lower the temperature in this climate of diseased lemons where the river radiates a nostalgic smell of molten mud. I don't care if the shoreline is asleep in dreams of dancing feathered cannibals. O the esplanades are endless equators of filth! And I am fated to wallow in these cancerous tropics! At least it is a pleasant season in hell, a dalliance in an oblivious paradise of brine and chemicals I would never deign to repent.

Field Marks

Finally! Lamps burst in sonic blooms of European light! O catalogue of
Bavarian kitsch, drape me in fuller sleeves. Just follow the instructions, get on
the barricades and blur the boundary between parachute and submarine. Let
me swallow the black stone. Demand the perfect absinthe column, an elaborate
hoax to convince the world to drink the juice-box of a strange city. Just let me
zig through this ziggurat, then we should burn burn the midnight-blue flame
and not awake to see the light of day elegant as a gleaming steel sculpture
against the backdrop of a nightclub where dancers set themselves aflame.

Of Passages and Reservoirs

I wanted to keep bottle up in air as long as possible
Not against floral patterned backdrop,
But you better be when I get back or I won't be will I?
In atrium's aquatic grape lights,
The more intimate original,
An argument I cannot possibly win.
Perhaps you weren't giving the night sky your full attention because your eyes
Were distracted.
But I was a clean slate,
A thing of the past.
Who else would dazzle us wearing three outfits at the same party?
When I leave the room, is this religion coincidence?
You asleep, blue baby in the Virgin's arms?
Could be hiding beneath otherwise smooth skin.
I didn't do any dropping in,
Transparency of the damp base of the tooth,
My nameless crocodile.

Blue Fragment

Like a fiery bed, I wait.
Turning over, I crash
into perpetual night.
The shop spits out a phantom businessman.
Looming is
persistence of lions,
birth of lagoon.
I find myself at sea level,
projected on the penthouse.
Please come
out on the circular dance floor
framed by the new highways.
There is no secret gluten.
Feed me.
There, like soap
is carted off in trucks.
O majestic sheet of steel,
flat surface of the water,
like what the body lacks.

Odalisque

I am haunted,
haunted by a boneless wraith of luminous black,
bent blue at the waist in the gestures of bathing.
Focusing and adjusting, I break the white grid around the contours of the body.

Let's go,
let's dance the pale cyclamen line,
the line of our selves and our loves that barely breathes its labored breath
beneath the onramp's protective ring of fire.

We vanish in a wave of heat,
a profusion of oranges and lemons.

It is easy to hold in the mind
the lover's damp brow, the chromatic veins
through indigenous skin, like the wilt of a sickly plant,

but the self is quite small
like a martyr, stretched out like tracing paper.

Square of Glass Ablaze

Brother, don't cry. Trip softly on these borrowed feet. There is no escaping the cruelly swelling asphalt. Perhaps the beautiful colored lights will save us. Early in the morning, we will find land. Early in the morning, we will meet our fate beyond this vast world of water. In winter the runways will become one long skating rink. The bluish milk will overlay the pavilion. I will never leave behind the museum of dark obelisks and Egyptian buttocks. The pity of it is that it moves me so. O martial monuments! O teak-lined boathouse! O empty landscape spread beneath the steel supports of a railway bridge! Must I sink still deeper in the quicksand to become aware of myself? Must the buildings stand in triplicate with fins? The glow of strange insects swarms through the night sky. Their iridescence provokes tears in me, and everything I see is filled with grease. I wind up in a taxi alone to ride to the last houses standing, the last panoramas.

The Makeshift Screen

In those same bake shops where we used to get drunk—the newspapers powdered with cocoa dust—I would pray for the smoky petrol stink of the underpass: trade a desired state for an undesired one. The lacy gathered shoulder straps took on repulsive shapes. That pale shadow of a neckline, dimly shot from blue benzene backdrop of a loaded pistol. One last traipse across the roller rink into the nightmare of an Antarctic childhood. I am almost at the mesa of Manhattan, the feathered coastline of an ancient and misgotten trust. Did we walk through the garden of an apartment complex to get there, to reach the restaurant in an abandoned subway station? The black skin seemed to expand almost endlessly, pushing its radius one bubble further at a time—seams tightening with soot. Our footsteps melded with the rubble. Which shoes were separate from the pile of boots beneath them? The window frames were lined with the pulp of softened wood. In the middle of the display: a book bound in a purple wrapper. Is it only a forgery of the book I want to read? Some bird of prey might peek out from a lamppost to nuzzle me, flash the bloodstained muzzle of its calloused foot. Should I try to part the bangs and force my way into the unlined forehead? Like the surface of a light bulb we are lit from beneath. O vague twilight of the half-lit stubbled chin! The litany of whitish lips until the street unloads its dark Pentecost. Oh, it's a situation that presents uncertainty. I see the wreckage from the corner of my eye. I will grind the fine powder where the faces start to reemerge from the wet wood of the shingles.

Solitaire

I wear my t-shirts
like a broken man,
tipping over cigarette
machines. O winter days!
My heart is spent on phone
calls to the beyond. The calliope
is the welcome disharmony
of our pirate ancestors.
O thread the buttonhole
with razorblades! The science
experiment has gone awry. The school
is burning quietly down, and no one
cares about the history
of each tattoo upon the arm.
The colors add dimensions to the chains.

Elephants by Satellite

Bird might visit, goldfish turn blue. I dance on the toes.
I know lamb coat with marmot trim. In the street, wind blows,
mist comes off the body. I turn blind eye so fish might come out. Royal blue
shoes be made especially for me. I see face against neck like a deep jungle, hard
not to see, full of the shadowy neutrino.

The Sub-ambient Blue is a Skylight

Wearing a suit of thin blue paper,
I burst through the white skin of the building.

Leaving only one shoe behind, I work
my way into the interior insulation.

O shoe I left behind.
Devices are born, grow old, and die.

Never will the bicycle give me peace.
Make way for the animals that do not shed tears,

the deer whose antlers incorporate the suede of boots,
the tiger whose skin mimics the flowers on the wallpaper.

We can work our way to the green flag of Sunday.
Let's take to the sky, leaving only a thin layer of snow behind.

Blue Eyedrops Instantly Whiten Bloodshot Eyes

Bookshop sells little orange book

so fast it's meaningless.

Raid the closet.

Oh lord no.

I don't blame any one for stealing them at all.

When I am quietly seated,

panels vibrate still.

Trigger me to go

to the line along which sun passes.

Blue rectangles.

It's an oscillation

from glass gallery.

Pinkish brown smudges.

Transparent sections in floor.

Beautiful vaulted hall with blue staircase.

Much stressed in media.

It wasn't for me.

I ask for better place.

Polyurethane

Bombs explode the half-closed matchbooks as the third trimester of pimentos folds the faithful in its hands. Blue star short-circuits the fat rosette of bar tabs. The zest of flesh beneath the transoms ignites the green neon of nocturnal limes. The telephone unfurls the pat coincidences of night-shift receptionists. The switchboard streams its smoke. But my eye is caught three times by the glint of fresh-washed dishes. My index finger prints the passport of tomorrow's abstract paydays.

Galerie des Machines

What a moment! No one will ever again stoke the flame of uncompromised wonder. No seraphic swan will find the grey cornice to roost on. And yet I am only killing time, waiting to find the inevitable baleen buried in the sand, the shattered scrimshaw. If I had been asked then, I would have wanted to be remembered as some insignificant molecular shimmer, as if that would be French enough! I remember only those brief moments in vegetative corners of darkened patios. The Hotel Le Cirque wanted to shake us out of our heavy sleep on these streets forever tattered now. What spectacular blue bug might awake from within this rotten pile of accordions! How gleefully we might welcome him and all his baroque pincers. The past holds some vague memory of a rescue at sea, but now the glisten of wet gravel is the sequin festooning our sorrow. It's no personal abyss I know! Collectively we rebel against it: the poignant splicers, the clutch of vertigo from the heights of the spinning hotel bar. Yet below me alone stretches the delirious landscape of dead stone. I am condemned to scale flight after flight of marble stairs, a torture designed by some cruel urban planner, no doubt. My heart could expect no less in this land of dodos, my concrete casket. But perhaps I only swoon to strike that final pose of pale and heartless beauty. It rains... rains. I am a creature who cannot rest until I disrupt the camouflage of my fevered raincoat. The clouds finally explode into an orange spider that dips its feet into the swollen river. Downstream, the streetcars shed their green metallic wrappers.

White

Pleasures of My Country

I am lost again in thoughts of torsos at the lumberyard, near misses of the early dawn. Should I breathe the vagrant curlicues of excommunicated inhalations? Is it too soon to introduce the wooden Bonaparte? Are we the same in stupid aspirations, leaving footprints in the tar? Let's sing librettos incognito until the phony mustache falls to reveal our true identity as barons of the loathsome word.

Talisman Against the Day

The backwards letters of the hotel marquee disintegrate in the broken sermons of the whammy bar. This fragment of the day is lost to the useless excavation of divine rubbish, the sweat-soaked gabardine of pilgrims and the assorted poker chips of prewar casinos. The roads seem unfamiliar, and the groom-to-be is snoring in the driver's seat at the precise moment I need his undivided attention. I'll leave behind a trail of broken cue sticks to find my way back. The river's just another ordinary baptism.

Dream of Fire

O sacristy of sodden songs! We chant the factory of youthful eyes awash in paper chains and cherry stems where ear lobes are adorned with bells and the prominence of bridges flattens yet another foot beneath the statue of this city's patron saint who moans astride the crescent of her tinseled racing bike which trails the flags of Abu Dhab and other emirates. Where else will Hammond organs plunk their Leslie wheels into the silt of aged rivers? Will the oil and sand of the machines of ancient industry re-anoint the piety of our infirm hearts?

Dream of Velvet Popes

We point the fingers of our afterthoughts like reduced facsimiles of faith.
Should we clang the timbalinas of the silver-plated renegades? O pomp and
poof of well-coiffed boutonnières! Shall we meander through the labyrinth of
prayer flags? Shall we suspend the turbine of remote-controlled guitars? Let's
pirouette on cast-iron feet. Let's down the frozen jiggers of antiquarian punk.
Let's rearrange the breathless sugar cane, our sweaters clasped to chests. Let's
dance the stripèd minotaur of Japanese fondue.

Wave After Wave

I am afraid of the heavily polished stone. It is as if I am shipwrecked on an abandoned cantilever bridge. Abandoned in violence or delight. By violence, of course, I do not mean the brutality of the circumlunar haze of light. In 2004 Luna Park too goes up in flames. So we all must wound what we love. The aquarium grows more debased with every new season. How disgusted I am of the garish penguin exhibit. My fuselage is all that remains. How I long for a propeller or a bit of cockpit! I am lost! Camel through a needle's eye. True bubble and squeak of my heart! How Biblical! I see smoke rising above the corpses of secretaries. I bend to kiss their waterlogged fingers and salvage what typewriters I can. What else can I do among these landlocked lighthouses? Ships are guided into the porticos of cathedrals. City Hall is split by the mizenmast of an antique schooner. Perhaps I am only involved in an oblique way. When I think of the bowling alley, buried in sand, the stripe-necked pins floating out to sea, what has it to do with me? The salted air is bitter; must my tongue now meet its winter? O beautiful fortress of bottle caps, you are almost up to my kneecaps. The Sirens lure me to a junction of highways and decaying filling stations to slowly anesthetize me with their Icelandic song. I will not a drop to drink. I will drink only of the skyline's neon pediments. I am waiting for the Cadillacs to rupture into bloated metal stingrays.

Atom Parlor

Beneath the gris-gris filigree of rusted out rotundas, we sat for several minutes at Osiris' feet. Infinite streams of mathematical solutions circled in the air. O dizzy spells of cigarette paper! Will laughter ring through quasi-glacial passages? O damp blouses of the rainy afternoon like prayers! O hopeless honeycomb! The French language distinguishes between the shades that cloud our sleep. Should we hopscotch to the amateur ballads of spontaneous physics? O nest of cherubs! The zest of easy tigers recaptures the sun. A hotel in the foreground is on fire, as the outlaws sing the tuneless radio in mythic voices. We are swearing in the second world of sound.

Quadregesima

The ocean taxidermy of the streets like milk in the morning of a city where a subway is in the works. Would it be natural to rearrange the freestyle alchemy of long nights at the craps table, the weather patterns of the region? The labels of the nipples just underground, out of sight. Here are the trinkets of a thousand Aztec cognoscenti, the ice deposits of the bouncers at certain ghastly bars where patrons predict the slapstick of asteroidal tragedy, where the pixelated lips of minor oracles inebriate the sewage, where we fall in love with hairlines that insinuate the gravitas of surf guitar. Even the lemonade is comatose. The epicenter shakes off all importance. The fortune-tellers cast aside fur coats.

Bird's Eye View

I am a prisoner of this building, hostage of this jalapeño haze. What else does the sun have in store for us? What newest dome of fire will eclipse the sky? I will take credit for every rhinestone, each vein on the back of the hand. My wristwatch shimmers but doesn't tell time. I am faced with a small chrome self, an unexpected titanium version of me that beeps and burps where I would sing. And maybe everything is becoming more mechanical. The waiters linger outside the restaurant like spaceships waiting permission to dock. Should I take to the streets strewn with discarded foosball tables, where houses fly their pirate flags? I don't mean for every face to dissolve around me, to retreat from the plume of white smoke. Yesterday I tried to reach everyone I knew on the phone. Tonight I wish I could forget the billboards and let my peninsula drift to some ocean beyond the crumbled bits of doughnut on the sidewalk outside my front door.

Bright White

Spine forced into a slight curve on a torso
that footlights cast shirtless shadows across.

It is terrible. Valley obscured by clouds, ribs aloof, generous white
patch on aerial maps. A slab of water appears to float in space.

I take a razor to the gray coat,
am a petty bandit of fading flesh.

There is so much space, so much blue, the silvery world
which is actually only a gesture, a kiss on the palm,
cold cheeks on the black background of the sky.

Steeped in white, feet slide and lurch like mechanical fish,
bright and slender through a magnetic field.

I take a detour over the tall steppes.
I send the postcard in transparent flaming patterns.

Possibility of Apocalypse

The door won't be open to the polar night. What white expanses will not spread before my feet! If ice should curl around my toe and ride the bloodstream to my lung, what stalagmite will tear the hole which absolves me of this boredom? Increasingly I see the human form as a ship lost to the ocean floor. I am condemned to troll the rancid streets for new love: the tattooed forearms under the cornices of hideously ornate skyscrapers. Lamppost after unlit lamppost. I dream up coffins beneath the snow banks. Each contains a beloved pet. A paper mask beclouds my lips in gauze. There is no time to grieve, only to make an escape past the refrigerated trucks. I am beckoned by the mechanical, the hum of distant pistons reminiscent of my saddest dreams. Slipped away into abandoned corners of the city where towers half-drowned by the shadows shrink toward the waist to end in a small black triangle. What now? Will hope invade this image like the flock of pigeons frightened by an explosion? Will a burst of light reveal the streets magically cleared of debris? If we go out onto the balcony now, we will see it: the black fog that denies the human body, the children below who are weeping over the wreckage of pinball machines—please forgive them!

Great Firefly Mouth

Our question says "river"
The river we see
I put on my gas mask
One in a series of gas masks
O dear pale skin of the wrist
Breathe up
Be done before
hat falls
Touch the belly like a broken temple
so that nothing may remain

Triumph of Aged Luchadors

Leave the Amazon of coral reefs to the wild yeast of heartbeats, the luminous carbonate of the body. The bones of exotic fish are calling out through Indonesian canopies as we drape our backs in the brocade reveille of homemade Haitian flags. The prophets of tobacconists predict the painted eyelines of heraldic glee. Should we wear the tattered veils of tattooed saints and beat the bongos of the paisley hermitage? The click of crimson castanets is the clack of tumbling continents. The wounded fingers that we slammed in restroom doors are signals of our struggle.

Pool Hall Quartet

Should I listen to the motorcycle's familiar rumble, the menace of the dying day? It is this and other hells I find myself condemned to, the orange smudge and squiggle of the horizon like a dark body, like the ghostly jingle of an unknown bell. And my city lies beneath the haze of clouds, dank and teeming with drunk cellists scraping their way through labyrinths of cobblestone. Is it me or do all these buildings look the same, each decked with paisley scarves? It hardly seems likely—the third dwarf I've seen today—or is it a toy elephant peeking through the sails? He is scared of his own invisibility, just like me. People only point me out to note the sloop of my shoulders, the silver of my frontispiece. My heart is wearing a sombrero and I almost don't know where to begin. My eyes are melding into one huge monster eye that will leave me Cyclopean and groping for my ancient home.

On the Grand Boulevards

I don't have time to think of things.
I see you disappear into the vegetation,
your turquoise camouflage,
diagonal of light across the green face.
It is no longer the sea.
I managed to slip in everything
between outside and inside,
between one space and another,
as the manta ray sings quietly for us
in the infinite consistency of ice.
We are frozen in time. The patterns of shadow
become skin and hair. Your throat becomes easily
the blue transparency of polished metal.
I think of the glint of weapons,
the hovering clouds of a frescoed dome.
It slits me like a bullet and I cannot sleep.

Skymap

Unending corridors of steel,
the blue diaphany of a corpse laid out on a slab
foamed with translucent blood.
I will make a map, denser and more useful,
overlapping circles of billboards and roofs.
Near pristine coastal zones I spent my life
burying a treasure several people have been sure they can locate.
Can they plug the sprig of basil from my chest?
The x-ray opened such a big hole.
Come in. Zip around my interior pockets
until my lip or body shimmers from your pressed powder,
I can scuttle my ship approximately
until I am pulled by the height of it,
no longer voided by the forcefulness I'm lacking,
making a fist around the spoons,
I feed myself with cilantro and coarse salt.
Let me turn toward each of the white blouses.
Let me crush plants tramping.
Let me pet a hummingbird in the open desert.
Let me give up packaged beef.
Let me sleep softly,
for morning is coming to an end.
Let me turn my outstretched hand towards the light.

Made in the USA
Charleston, SC
07 March 2010